STEPHANIDES BROTHERS'
GREEK MYTHOLOGY

SERIES A: THE GODS OF OLYMPUS   No. 3

The original Greek edition of this book has been approved by the Hellenic Ministry of Education as a supplementary reader.

APOLLO AND HIS LYRE
APOLLO · HERMES

Retold by MENELAOS STEPHANIDES
Illustrated by YANNIS STEPHANIDES

Translation: BRUCE WALTER

SIGMA PUBLICATIONS
20, MAVROMIHALI ST., 106 80 ATHENS GREECE, TEL: 210 3607667, FAX: 210 3638941
www.sigmabooks.gr
e-mail: sigma@sigmabooks.gr

APOLLO AND HIS LYRE

1st edition 1977
7th edition 2005

Printed by «Fotolio», bound by Dedes Dionysis and Co.

Copyright © 2005: Sigma Publications - Menelaos Stephanides - Yannis Stephanides
All rights reserved throughout the world
Published and printed in Greece.
ISBN 960-425-017-5

APOLLO

Long, long ago, when Zeus ruled over gods and men, the sacred island of Delos was not fixed in its present position in the archipelago of the Cyclades. In those times it was a floating island, drifting endlessly over seas and oceans – until one day a goddess set foot upon its shores, fear and anguish written upon her face. Her name was Leto. In her womb she bore two of Zeus' children, Apollo and Artemis, and now she was seeking a place where she could give birth.

"O island," cried the goddess, "age-long wanderer upon the waves, give me refuge and let me bear my children on your soil. I have been hunted all over the world by the Python, the fearsome monster which jealous Hera sent after me to seek revenge. I have been to Attica and to Thrace, to Lesbos, Chios – everywhere. Nowhere will they let me give birth. They all fear the terrible Python and the wrath of Hera. Receive me now, o island, you who know what endless wandering means, and I promise you that

LETO ON DELOS

Apollo, the son whom I shall bear, will raise on your soil a splendid temple that will make your name renowned."

Hardly had these words passed Leto's lips when a violent trembling shook the whole of Delos. Two huge rocks thrust themselves upwards from the sea bed and the island settled firmly upon them, fixing itself once and for all in the position where it lies today. Thus Delos received Leto.

THE BIRTH OF APOLLO

Immediately, a host of other goddesses came to Leto's aid. Nine whole days and nights she was in labour and when, on the tenth night, she finally bore her children, the darkness immediately turned to bright daylight and the sun appeared in majesty in the heavens, casting its golden beams upon the isle. Truly, it could not have been otherwise, for the son that she bore was the god of light, golden-haired Apollo; and with him was born stern Artemis, goddess of moonlit nights.

Four days passed and already Apollo was a lithe youth filled with immortal power. When Hephaestus made him a gift of a silver bow with golden arrows that could not miss their mark, the young god resolved to kill the Python, the monster that had pursued his mother so relentlessly.

Swift as lightning, Apollo flew to Parnassus, where the dreadful monster had its lair. Until that moment, nobody had dared to raise his arm against the Python, which spread unheard-of miseries all around it. Wherever it dragged its serpent's body the earth and all its fruits decayed and a foul rottenness spread over the land, whilst men died immediately they set eyes upon its awful form.

As soon as the fearsome dragon realized that someone had dared to try his strength against it, it came out of its lair and wormed its huge length among the rocks, searching out the enemy. When the monster saw that the being who stood before it

APOLLO SLAYS THE PYTHON

was none other than the child of Leto, it went mad with anger and flecks of foam dripped from its mouth in its fury. Raising itself upon its snaky coils the Python loomed threateningly over Apollo, drawing its head back for the lunge that would tear the young god into bloody pieces.

Quicker than lightning, Apollo loosed a single arrow at the Python and hit it straight between the eyes.

A terrifying howl echoed through the mountain gorges as the horrible monster, mortally wounded, beat its writhing scales against the rocky slopes of Mount Parnassus, coiling and then uncoiling to its full length. Suddenly it raised itself, huge and threatening, to its full height only to fall back again with a fearful thud which shook the whole mountain. The Python was dead.

Overjoyed by his great victory, Apollo took up his beloved golden lyre and began to sing the paean of victory. To the triumph of a heroic feat was added yet another triumph, a triumph that was no more than a song, but a song so wonderful the world had never heard its like before. From its words and music sprang all the contrast between savage struggle and peace, between destruction and creation, death and life. It was a song of overwhelming beauty and power, a song which nature heard in silent awe and which filled the eyes of oppressed mankind with tears of trembling happiness.

When Apollo's paean had ended, a mighty clamour rose up on all sides. It was the tumultuous cheers and delighted cries of mankind and all nature, their roars of applause at this triumphant hymn; and ever since, he has rightly held unchallenged the title of god of music.

Apollo buried the Python on the side of Mount Parnassus and over the monster's grave he built a temple and an oracle. This was the sacred oracle of Delphi, which reveals to men the judgements of almighty Zeus, Apollo's father.

THE PAEAN OF VICTORY

THE SHEPHERD OF KING ADMETUS

The Python, however, was the son of mother Earth, and in killing it Apollo had become a murderer. Since Apollo was the very god who would one day hold the power to absolve repentant killers of their sins, his first duty was to cleanse himself from the guilt of his own crime, even though it had been a blessing to gods and men alike. And so, casting off his immortal form, he went to Thessaly, where he became a humble shepherd in the service of king Admetus of Pherae. Thus the golden-haired youth tended the royal flocks, and nobody, not even Admetus himself, suspected that the young herdsman was Apollo, god of light.

Yet strange things would happen whenever Apollo took his master's herds to graze. Whenever the god picked up his lyre and let his fingers play upon its strings, the wild beasts would come out of the forest as if entranced and gambol around him joyfully, mingling with the cows and sheep. From the time of Apollo's arrival, wealth and happiness began to flow into the courts of Admetus. His flocks multiplied, his store-rooms filled with sacks of grain, and his great urns overflowed with olives and wine, oil and butter. From the walls and roofbeams hung heavy bags of cheese, legs of ham and other foods, all of the choicest quality.

Handsome young Admetus rejoiced in the plenty that he saw around him. Mounted upon his white stallion, he would ride out over the plain, admiring his herds, his sleek and well-muscled horses galloping over the rolling turf and his powerful oxen dragging

the plough deep through the fertile soil.

Many kings now wanted Admetus as their son-in-law and offered him their daughters; but he loved only Alcestis, the lovely daughter of Pelias, king of neighbouring Iolchus.

Pelias, however, had no intention of marrying his daughter off, for who else was there to tend him in his old age? So he declared that he would only give his daughter away to a man who could harness a lion and a wild boar to his chariot.

How could anyone yoke together two wild beasts so different and so savage when till now no one had even dared try yoking one alone? Admetus, however, was so emboldened by his love for the sweet Alcestis that he was willing to risk being torn to pieces by the savage beasts. And when Apollo heard of his brave decision, he resolved to help him and gave him the strength he would need to achieve his aim.

Thus the daring Admetus performed the mighty feat Pelias had demanded, and now he was thundering along the road to Iolchus, his chariot harnessed to a lion and a wild boar.

Overcome with awe at the brave young man's incredible feat, Pelias handed over his daughter without protest. Alcestis took her place in the chariot and Admetus brought her in triumph back to his palace, where a sumptuous wedding was celebrated.

ADMETUS ACHIEVES THE IMPOSSIBLE

Nine years Apollo had bound himself to serve Admetus, and when the ninth year drew to its close the golden-haired god returned to Delphi, purified at last. From then on, Apollo was to be the god of the great and noble ideal of forgiveness, offering his protection to every man who showed sincere and true remorse.

Apollo liked to stay at Delphi, where now stood his majestic temple and the sacred oracle. Yet neither did he forget Delos, the island of his birth – and above all he did not forget the promise his mother, Leto, had made before she bore him. For this reason, it was not long before a gleaming temple, built by Apollo, stood out among the other sacred monuments of the island.

THE LAND BEYOND THE NORTH

But from time to time he would leave Greece to travel to the mythical sunlit land beyond the North where his mother now lived.

Apollo's journeys to this enchanting land were long but wonderful. Mounted on a winged chariot drawn by two great, snow-white swans, he would travel high above the clouds, leaving Greece far behind him. As he travelled further northwards, he would catch sight of the first snows from on high, covering the mountains peaks like white caps. Gradually the snow would grow thicker, until everything beneath Apollo's chariot seemed covered by a white sheet. But above the clouds, where Apollo flew, the weather was always spring-like, and the great swans would draw the chariot onwards swiftly and tirelessly. Finally, even further to the north, the snows would begin to thin out, and far beyond the pole itself golden sunbeams would shine through the clouds, shedding their light upon an enchanted land.

This was the land of the Hyperboreans, the Land Beyond the North. Here was a country of eternal spring, brightly coloured and bathed in cool light; a region echoing with the tinkle of plashing waters and the sweet songs of iridescent birds. As soon as the golden-haired god descended from his chariot and set foot upon the green grass the birds would burst into a frenzied song of welcome and flutter among the branches and the golden shafts of sunlight. So beautifully did they sing that their melody almost rivalled the heavenly notes that Apollo plucked from his lyre.

But at that same moment in distant Greece, clouds would darken the sky. Cold and rain would follow, for the god of light had left his homeland and dark winter was coming in his stead. Huddled around their fires, people would patiently await the return of Apollo and the winter's end. When the god of light came back he would chase away the dark days with his golden beams and bring in the warm and sparkling spring. Then people would hold great feasts to worship the god and sing songs about the sun, the light and the joys of life.

APOLLO AND DAPHNE

Apollo loved all life's beauties. One day, at Delphi, he was shooting at targets with his golden arrows. While he was practising, young Eros, the winged son of Aphrodite, arrived on the scene looking for a chance to enmesh Apollo in some affair of the heart.

Seeing that Apollo's arrow had just plunged into an apple hanging from a distant bough, Eros raised his bow and aimed it at the same target.

"Leave me alone, little boy, and let me shoot my arrows," said Apollo in annoyance, "and don't be rash enough to try your skill against mine."

"I know your arrows never miss, but mine, too, hit their mark," replied Eros, even more annoyed than Apollo; and with that he opened his wings and flew up onto the slopes of Mount Parnassus. There he drew two arrows from his quiver – one to arouse love and the other to make the beloved feel only fear and dislike. With the first arrow he wounded Apollo to the heart, and with the second he shot at the nymph Daphne, daughter of the river Peneius, who happened to be passing by at that moment.

Pierced by the dart of love, Apollo was dazzled by the nymph's lovely face and noble form and went over to speak to her.

Daphne, however, had been struck by the arrow which rejected love, and as soon as she saw him she moved further away. Then the golden-haired god came closer still; but with hasty steps she moved even further from him. With a few quick bounds, he tried once again to approach the lovely nymph. That was enough. Daphne took to her heels. Now Apollo ran after her as if possessed, crying to her to stop; but she ran ever swifter. Both Eros' arrows had found their mark.

"Stop, stop, I beg you," Apollo pleaded. "I don't wish to harm you." But the fleet-footed nymph continually evaded his clutches. However, he did not give up, and kept on running after her and begging her to stop.

"Don't be afraid, lovely nymph!" he called. "Why do you flee as if some wild beast were pursuing you? I am not evil. I am Apollo, the son of Zeus. Stop running like a frightened deer, I beg you!"

But Daphne kept on running. At times Apollo gained on her and it seemed that he would catch her, and at times she would surge ahead with a sudden bound. Then he would be hot on her heels again, reaching out to catch her, but again she would slip from his grasp like a terrified butterfly.

Yet the golden-haired god would not give up his wild pursuit. The dart of love had

DAPHNE FLEES

lit a fire within him which could not be quenched.

"She can't last out much longer. Sooner or later she will tire and I shall catch her," said Apollo to himself as he kept on running after the nymph.

Sure enough, Daphne eventually began to tire. Apollo drew nearer and nearer to her. Now he was stretching out his hands, now he was about to touch her, now she was almost in his grasp.

DAPHNE IS TURNED INTO A LAUREL

"O gods and mother Earth!" gasped Daphne, "why do you let me fall into Apollo's clutches? I do not want Apollo for my husband. I would rather become a rock or a tree than have Apollo touch me."

Hardly had Daphne spoken these words when her feet became rooted to the ground. From her hair and her arms sprang branches and leaves, while her body became the trunk of a tree. Thus the lovely nymph was transformed into a fragrant daphne bush, the familiar laurel of our own times, and instead of embracing her, Apollo found himself clutching an armful of leaves.

The golden-haired god was overcome with sorrow. He was grieved to think that the nymph with whom he had fallen in love so suddenly and so deeply had been lost on his account. With sad eyes, he fondled the foliage of the fragrant laurel and then broke off a spray of leaves to weave a garland for his brow. Apollo was never to forget the lovely and untameable nymph and that is why he is often shown wearing a circlet of

laurel leaves on his head.

Apollo never married. He was the most handsome of all the gods and lived his life exactly as he pleased. He did promise to marry on one occasion, but even then it was doubtful whether he would have remained faithful, and fortunately the wedding never took place.

APOLLO AND MARPESSA

The girl was Marpessa, daughter of the king of Aetolia. Her father, Evenus, treated her harshly, but he was a worthy and brave warrior.

He had announced that he would give his daughter only to the man who could beat him in a chariot duel.

Marpessa was so lovely, and her fortune so immense, that at first there were many who found the courage to meet Evenus single-handed; but each had been killed in his turn and now there was no one left who dared to face him – until one day a handsome and daring youth appeared before Marpessa mounted on a winged horse, a pegasus. He was the heroic Idas, son of the king of Messene, and he had never yet been defeated in battle.

Marpessa had heard many tales of Idas' feats and she was appalled when she saw

MARPESSA AND IDAS

him. Better not to be married at all than be wedded to the man who would slay her father; for now it would not just be any young warrior that Evenus would have to face, but the renowned hero Idas, who could certainly defeat him.

Idas saw the fear in Marpessa's eyes and he said gently:

"Listen, lovely princess. I have not come to kill your father and I want neither his wealth nor his throne. Come, let us leave secretly before day breaks."

When Marpessa heard the noble young man's proposal she was overwhelmed with joy, and immediately agreed to leave with him. He placed her on the back of his splendid pegasus, a gift from Poseidon, and they sped through the air towards Messene.

As soon as king Evenus learned that his daughter had fled with Idas, he called upon Apollo for aid. The god, who loved Marpessa himself, willingly agreed to help, and quick as lightning the two set off together in pursuit of the runaway lovers.

But as they were crossing the river Lycormas, Evenus was swept away by its turbulent waters. Apollo plunged in and dragged him out, but it was too late: Evenus was dead. Apollo swore over the king's body that he would take Marpessa from Idas and make her his wife. He also promised the dead king that although his life had been lost his name would remain immortal, for the river where he had been drowned would henceforth be called the Evenus. Having spoken these words, the god sped off once more in pursuit of Idas; and before the youth could reach the shelter of Messene he found himself face to face with Apollo.

Idas guessed immediately what the god had come for, but instead of retreating he quickly placed himself before Marpessa to shield her, whilst his grim expression showed that he was ready for whatever might come. The young man who had avoided a duel with Evenus, a mere mortal, did not now hesitate to pit his strength against a god. Within moments the two adversaries were locked in struggle.

It was a terrible fight. Although Idas was no god, he was stronger than a lion and he fought against Apollo as an equal. It was not long before Zeus noticed the disturbance, and he decided to part them. However, the two were locked in such furious combat that it seemed impossible to do so, and it was only when the lord of Olympus hurled a thunderbolt between them that he brought the fighting to a halt.

When they had scrambled to their feet, Zeus ordered them to tell him what the quarrel was about.

"Father Zeus," Apollo protested, "I want Marpessa for my wife and this mortal shows

IDAS FIGHTS APOLLO

THE JUDGEMENT OF ZEUS

great disrespect in daring to stand in my way."

"Father of gods and men," replied Idas, "Marpessa is mine, and nothing will make me give her up."

Zeus stood thoughtfully for a moment and then, turning towards Marpessa, said to her:

"Fair princess, you have every right to choose for yourself the husband whom you want, and I promise you that whatever you decide will be fulfilled."

Marpessa humbly thanked great Zeus for his ruling and then, turning to the god of light, she said:

"Apollo, you are a god and will enjoy eternal youth, but I shall grow old one day and then you will abandon me. Lord Zeus, for years I have lived in unhappiness, knowing that I was destined to be married to my father's killer. Of all my suitors, only Idas has shown love, discretion and indomitable courage. I love him and wish to become his wife."

And so it came about. Apollo submitted to the will of Zeus, and, filled with admiration for Marpessa's good sense and Idas' boldness, he wished them every happiness and departed for Delphi.

Apollo never knew sadness – for did he not have his lyre, which banished all troubles and brought him calm and joy? He would often play upon it at the great symposia of the gods on Olympus. When he touched his fingers to the magic strings

THE STRAINS OF THE GOLDEN LYRE

of the golden instrument, the nine Muses would run joyfully to his side and take up the song, and the whole place would echo with sweet, immortal melodies. And when they were in the mood for dancing, the Muses and the Graces would spring up at once and with them the lovely Aphrodite; but first in line would be Apollo's sister, graceful Artemis.

And as spirits rose on Olympus, so unhappiness faded from the earth.

Apollo also had some children, one of whom was Pan, the goat-footed god of the woods; but of him we shall tell in a later book. Another of his sons was the renowned physician, Asclepius.

His mother was Coronis, daughter of the king of Thessaly, but she died as soon as she had given birth to him. Apollo then placed the child in the care of the wisest teacher in the world, the centaur Cheiron who lived on the thickly-wooded slopes of Mount Pelion. Under Cheiron's guidance, Asclepius learned so much of medicine that in the end his knowledge surpassed even that of his teacher. Not only was there no illness he could not cure, but he had even learned the secret of restoring life.

ASCLEPIUS

However, this was a blessing men were not destined to enjoy for long, for Pluto, lord of Hades, complained to his brother Zeus about this raising of the dead, fearing that if it continued the Kingdom of the Underworld would soon be emptied.

When the lord of Olympus heard that the dead were being brought back to life, he sprang to his feet in a rage. His brows darkened, his eyes took on a fierce glint and immediately the sky was filled with black clouds.

Lightning flashed, thunder rolled and the earth began to shake. It was as if all the heavens were tumbling down.

"Who is he to change the established order and the laws which govern the world?" roared the lord of gods and men; and instantly he struck Asclepius down with a thunderbolt and sent him to the kingdom of Hades.

Apollo was grieved at the loss of his son, but his death was mourned even more by the mortal men who had worshipped him above many of the gods.

However, even from the underworld Asclepius still had the power to help mankind and cure the sick, and all over Greece there were temples in his honour and other buildings, called "asclepeia", which were a kind of hospital and were always built in the healthiest spot in each region. There the priests of Asclepius, who were also physicians, cured the sick by consultation, with herbal medicines and through prayer.

Asclepius was helped in his work by his daughters Hygeia and Panacea. The first of these made sure that people lived in a healthy way, to avoid illness, whilst the second was a wonderful pharmacist. She had compounded a medicine the like of which was nowhere to be found. It, too, was called the panacea. It was a very rare medicine, but it cured every disease – or so people said.

HERMES

Now we come to the most devious of the gods, crafty Hermes, the son of Zeus and Maia. Hermes was born in a cave on lofty Mount Cyllene in Arcadia, and as soon as he saw the light of day he began his cunning tricks. As he was a god there was no need for years to pass until he could prove his powers, and so he was up to mischief even before he was out of his cradle.

Nobody knows what Apollo had done to Hermes to put the idea of stealing his cattle into the young god's head. Whatever it was, little Hermes clambered out of his cradle and set off for Piereia where Apollo was tending the herds of the gods of Olympus.

With great stealth and cunning, Hermes managed to rob Apollo of fifty heifers without being seen and to lead them off to the Peloponnese. And what sly means did he not employ to bring his feat to a successful conclusion! Before he had gone very far, he prised the hooves from the heifers' feet and stuck them on again back to front; then he flung his sandals into the sea and quickly made himself another pair with pointed heels and rounded toes. Thus, anyone who followed the marks on the road would think that the herd and the person driving them were going in the direction the footprints showed, whilst it was really quite the opposite.

HERMES STEALS APOLLO'S HEIFERS

THE MEETING WITH THE OLD MAN

Further down the road, young Hermes met an old man. Fearing that he might reveal his secret, the little god gave the old man a heifer and told him:

"If you saw something, pretend you saw nothing – and if you heard something, pretend you heard nothing, either. Agreed?"

"Agreed," replied the old man, more than happy with the heifer he was offered for his pains.

Hermes set off down the road once more, but he was still none too happy about the old man.

"He could give the whole game away," said the young god to himself. "I had better go back and see if he is as good as his word." And so, having hid the heifers in a wood, Hermes transformed himself into a hunter, went back to the old man and said:

"Tell me which way a young boy went with fifty cows, and I shall give you an ox and a heifer."

The old man liked the idea of this second gift and all unsuspecting showed the "hunter" the way they had gone.

"Traitor!" shouted Hermes, "now I'll show you whom you're dealing with!" As he spoke, the earth shook and a huge rock broke loose from the mountainside and flattened the old man beneath it. Believe it or not, the rock was the very image of the old man – except that it could no longer betray confidences!

If ever you go down to the Peloponnese, perhaps you may see a rock whose shape reminds you of that story of the old man. And if it is not the rock which crushed him, then, who knows, perhaps it is at least the rock which gave rise to the legend.

But to return to our story.

After punishing the old man, Hermes went back to the wood, rounded up the herd, and finally drove them to a place near Pylos. There he slaughtered two heifers as an offering to the gods. But where was the fire to roast them on? It didn't take the quick-witted youngster very long to find an answer to that. He took two bone-dry laurel twigs and rubbed them together until they burst into flame. Then he spitted the two heifers and put them on the fire to roast. When they were done, he divided the meat into ten portions and offered one to each of the other gods – except Apollo, of course! Who would dare give him away, now that all Olympus had shared in the spoils? Hermes himself ate nothing; he just sniffed the savoury odours from the roasting meat and that was enough for him.

Once the sacrifice was completed, he hid the remaining heifers in a cave and then went quietly and happily back to his cradle.

As soon as his mother saw him, she began to scold him for having been away all day; but young Hermes was quite unabashed and proudly told her of the cunning trick he had played.

"You silly child," cried Maia, "aren't you afraid of Apollo? Don't you know his arrows

never miss their mark? What have you done?"

"I'm not afraid of Apollo," replied the little god, "and if he tries to make a fuss about this, I'll go and loot his temple at Delphi – and then you'll see how everybody laughs at him!"

Apollo, of course, soon realised that his heifers had gone, and began searching for them. On looking around, he quickly found the hoofmarks of the heifers and with them the footprints of a child. He followed them, but saw to his surprise that the marks were leading him back to his starting point. It never occurred to him that a thief could possibly be so cunning, and as he could think of no other way of getting at the truth he decided to consult the oracles. He was the most skilled of all the gods in interpreting them, and it was he who had built the oracle at Delphi. The signs told Apollo that it was Hermes who had stolen his heifers and that they were hidden in a cave near Pylos. Apollo hastened to the spot, and once more found hoofmarks outside the cave and the footprints of the same child. But the marks all showed that the cave was now empty and the heifers had gone.

"He got here before me and took them away," thought Apollo, and, deceived once more by the reversed footprints, he didn't go into the cave at all.

Anxious not to waste another moment, Apollo took a mighty leap and within seconds had reached Cyllene, where he found Hermes lying in his cradle.

GET UP, THIEF!

"Tell me where you've hidden the heifers!" Apollo roared. "Tell me this very instant or I'll throw you into the darkest depths of Tartarus!"

But what hope was there of getting a straight answer from the cunning little god? Young Hermes just acted like a baby and replied innocently, "Don't expect me to know where they are – I was only born yesterday!"

But Apollo did not believe a word crafty Hermes was saying.

"Get up, you little thief!" he shouted furiously. "I'm taking you off to Zeus this minute. You won't get away with any more of your cunning tricks, just you see!"

Hermes, however, just lay where he was, while Apollo grew more and more angry. Finally, losing all patience, he dragged the baby god from his cradle and carried him off in the direction of Olympus.

"All right, all right," cried Hermes. "There's no need to treat me like this. I didn't say I wouldn't go." And as soon as Apollo had put him down, he added craftily, "And when we get there, you'll see how wrong you were to call me a thief."

They soon found Zeus, but even when faced by the lord of Olympus, his own and Apollo's father, Hermes boldly denied all knowledge of the theft.

"You know yourself," he told Zeus, "that I didn't take Apollo's heifers."

Zeus most certainly did know, and in a stern tone that put a stop to all argument he ordered Hermes to take Apollo that very instant to the spot where the heifers were hidden.

THE COMMAND OF ZEUS

THE GREAT SURPRISE

What else could Hermes do? Zeus was in no mood for joking – so he took Apollo and led him to the cave near Pylos.

Apollo looked down and once more saw the hoofmarks which showed that the heifers had gone. He turned to Hermes with a suspicious look and said,

"I see you're still trying to pull the wool over my eyes." Then he lost his temper and shouted:

"Take me to the place where you've really hidden those heifers or I'll..."

"Calm down, calm down!" Hermes told him in a soothing tone, "and come inside." And taking Apollo by the hand he led him into the cave.

Apollo could hardly believe his eyes when he saw the herd standing there. Who would have believed such cunning existed? To be fooled by a babe in arms! Scarlet with wounded pride and rage, he could hardly keep his hands from the little god, but Hermes, behaving as if nothing had happened, picked up a strangely-shaped lyre and began to play a melody of such beauty that the infuriated Apollo, who was, remember, the god of music, immediately forgot to be angry and listened as if spellbound.

"What heavenly notes come from this strange instrument!" he marvelled. "What Muse is this that calms all passions and dispels anger with such ease?"

But if the music had moved Apollo, it exerted an even greater influence upon

Hermes himself. He felt a change take place within him. He now felt ashamed of his crafty behaviour and said:

"I shouldn't have done that to you."

Then he offered Apollo his lyre and added, "Please take this lyre to show that you're not still angry with me. I made it with my own hands. I took an empty tortoise shell and fixed these strings to it. You heard how beautifully it plays!"

For the god of music this was the most precious gift he could have wished for. So great was Apollo's joy that he swore that none of the immortal gods would ever be so dear to him as Hermes. Their joy was mutual; for when Hermes gave his lyre to Apollo he felt as if he were giving him a part of himself. The feeling made him very happy, for he knew that friendship is won by giving.

When the time came for them to part, Apollo stood in thought for a moment and then said:

"Hermes, take the heifers. I want you to have them as a gift. Please, if you want to seal our friendship, don't refuse them." And so they parted, delighted with the

A FRIENDSHIP IS BORN

**HERMES
THE GOD OF COMMERCE**

exchange.

Thus ended Hermes' first wicked prank. Yet it was not to be the only one, for the young god simply could not stay out of mischief. Once he took Poseidon's trident and hid it; another time he stole Ares' sword; and once he even dared to hide his father's sceptre. If Zeus hadn't found it almost immediately who knows on whom he would have vented his anger.

Once however, when he was still a boy, Hermes learnt a painful lesson. He went to steal his father's thunderbolts, but as soon as he laid hands on them they burst into flame. There were great rolls of thunder and flashes of lightning. Young Hermes burnt his fingers and cried out in panic at the noise. But the crash of the thunderclaps was nothing to his father's angry roars. Hermes realised that he had done wrong and was thoroughly ashamed of having made such a fool of himself.

However, Hermes could also put his cunning to good use. In an earlier chapter we saw him steal back Zeus' tendons from the Typhoon and thread them into his father's hands and feet again, thus helping him to defeat the hideous monster.

The truth is that nobody could surpass Hermes in cunning, intelligence and swiftness. He had wings on his ankles and could fly to the furthest corners of the earth in a matter of seconds.

For this reason he was the messenger of the gods and at the special command of Zeus, who made frequent use of his abilities and assigned him the most difficult tasks. But whatever the lord of Olympus had set him to do, the quick-witted Hermes never had any difficulty in accomplishing the mission he had undertaken.

Being a wily god, Hermes had a special affection for wily men, and for this reason he was the patron of merchants and lawyers, who are well known for their guileful ways. With his herald's staff he bestowed wealth and happiness on those under his protection.

It was even said that he shielded thieves, but many of them came to an evil end, and then they blamed Hermes for leaving them to their fate.

Hermes also protected labourers, farm workers and especially shepherds, since, as we have seen, he acquired a herd of his own when he was still only a baby. Even the hat he wore was a herdsman's cap on which he had fastened wings.

As he was young, handsome and strongly

built, Hermes loved field sports. He was the patron of athletes and made sure that the rules were observed in all contests. This was why statues of Hermes were to be found by every running track.

At crossroads and half-way points along the main routes, travellers would come upon busts of Hermes mounted on pillars. There they could rest secure in the knowledge of his protection – for no robber would dare to attack a traveller resting at the foot of one of Hermes' columns.

HERMES AND TRAVELLERS

These columns had useful information for travellers inscribed upon them, which was of great assistance to any who had not been along the road before. There was also a thoughtful custom of leaving a little food for hungry travellers at their base.

In spite of his crafty tricks and his sly ways, Hermes was one of the most popular of gods with mortals and Olympians alike. There were many who even admired him for his little weaknesses, but he wanted people to be intelligent and clear-thinking, and to those who were he showed especial favour.

DAPHNIS THE SON OF HERMES

Hermes' quick mind and supple form made him the favourite of the wood-nymphs. One of the nymphs of Sicily bore him a son, but she was a heartless mother and abandoned her child in a grove of laurels, or "daphnes" as they are called in Greek.

Some kind water-nymphs found the baby among the laurels. They named him Daphnis, and brought him up with loving care to be a fine shepherd. Daphnis had a deep love of music and was taught to play the pipes by Pan, the goat-footed god of the woods. Daphnis made up his own songs and composed his own melodies, which he sang and played on the pan-pipes. In his verses he told of the life of the shepherd and the beauty of the forests and mountain pastures and thus he became the first pastoral poet. Hermes was very fond of his son Daphnis, for he was a young man who brought credit to his father's name and became known the world over for the melodies he played and the poems which he set to music.

This handsome and noble shepherd was loved by the nymph Lyce and they became the happiest and best matched couple in the whole of Sicily. For Lyce, too, had a lovely, sweet voice and when she sang and he played on the pipes it was as if

some muse from Olympus were singing and Pan himself were playing.

Yet although there was nothing to cast a shadow on their happiness, Lyce fell prey to a great fear – the fear that she would lose her beloved.

"Daphnis, dearest," she said, "the happier I feel, the more afraid I become. There are times when I can see our happiness collapsing in ruins. I am afraid of losing you, Daphnis, and I would rather die than have such a thing happen."

"Dearest love," replied Daphnis, "only the gods know our fate. If I should die, pray for a brave heart and struggle to live on; but for me to forget you while I live, why, that's impossible. I swear before the gods that I would let you blind me with your own hands if ever I should leave you for the sake of another woman."

Yet fate decreed that the very next day the impossible should happen.

Daphnis had gone out hunting, and, tired by the chase, sat down upon a stone to rest. Then he took up his pan-pipes and began to play a melody. Nearby, hidden behind the thick foliage of the forest trees, was a splendid palace. A gentle breeze wafted the sweet notes of Daphnis' pipes straight to the open window of the princess who sat there listening, enchanted by the beauty of music. When the last notes of the pipes had died away, the princess ran down the steps and stood in the palace gateway, hoping to catch sight of the musician. Meanwhile, Daphnis had got to his feet and had gone on through the forest in the mid-day heat, searching for water. Suddenly without realising it, he found himself before the palace gates, looking full in the face of the king's daughter, who had come forward at that very moment.

DAPHNIS AND LYCE

THE WATER OF OBLIVION

When she saw the handsome youth with his pipes, the princess fell in love with him on the spot and asked him to come up to the palace.

"Just bring me a little water to quench my thirst," replied Daphnis, "and then I'll be on my way, fair princess, for I am out past my time and my beloved awaits my return."

The princess, however, was no ordinary woman. She was well-versed in sorcery and into his water she poured a few drops of juice from the magic herb of forgetfulness.

She then came back to the gates and stretched out her arm with a smile to hand Daphnis the drink.

At that moment a sudden breeze blew up. The leaves rustled on the trees and in their murmuring it seemed as if a voice could be heard:

"No, Daphnis! Don't drink it! Don't you see her eyes? They are the eyes of a witch, Daphnis!"

But the young man's ears were filled with the sound of tinkling waters and he stretched out both hands to the cup.

"Daphnis! No, Daphnis!" came the voice again. "Do not drink the water of oblivion or you will forget us!"

"It must be the wind," said Daphnis to himself. "There's nobody here but the princess and me, and besides, I'm hot and thirsty and I want a drink." And tossing back his parched throat he emptied the cup in one draught.

Thus Daphnis quenched his thirst – and thus he forgot the girl he loved, his vow to the gods and everything else.

Taking him by the hand, the princess led him into the palace.

Lyce awaited his return in vain. Hour after hour went by, and then, desperate with anxiety, she began to search for him high and low. Eventually, quite by chance, she found herself outside the gates of the palace. Two guards stood there.

"I am looking for Daphnis, the singer with the pan-pipes," sobbed Lyce. "Have you seen him pass this way, by any chance?"

"Don't ask for Daphnis again. He is the princess's lover now, so forget him just as he has forgotten you," replied one of the guards, realising who Lyce was.

Like a mad creature, the nymph burst into the palace. Before anyone had time to stop her she was face to face with Daphnis.

Daphnis met her look. It was as if he had been struck by a thunderbolt which woke him from a dreadful nightmare.

"Lyce..." he stammered.

"The vow, the vow, o gods!" cried Lyce – and her eyes burned into the young man's as if they were flashing fire.

As Daphnis stared at her, his eyes opened wide in terror and as they did so, pains began to shoot through them. Soon the agony was unbearable, and instinctively he closed his eyes. When he opened them again he could no longer see.

DAPHNIS BLINDED

THE DEATH OF DAPHNIS

Now Daphnis was blind, and he picked his uncertain way through the woods playing sad melodies on his pipes and singing of the sweetest happiness in the world, which had turned into the bitterest sorrow.

Whilst wandering aimlessly one day, groping his way in the pitch darkness of high noon, he fell from a rock and was killed.

Hermes found his son as the breath was leaving his body, and carried him off to Olympus. And there at the foot of the rock, on the spot where he fell, a spring gushed forth. To this very day the people of Sicily point out this spring and say that in the plashing of its waters the pipes of Daphnis can be heard.

SOME ANSWERS TO POSSIBLE QUERIES

To those of our readers, young or old, whose reading of this mythology series may have prompted certain questions, we would like to say the following:

It is possible that you may have read the same myth elsewhere and noticed significant differences. This does not necessarily mean that one version is right and the other wrong. In their retelling, myths came to differ widely from place to place and from age to age and as a result several versions are now extant. In this work, we decided to give one version only, choosing either that most widely accepted, or the one we felt to have the most value. Working by the same criteria we have often added materials taken from other sources to round out a myth.

Another frequent cause of bewilderment are the contradictions generally encountered in mythology. For example, in one myth Zeus may be depicted as kind and fair, and in another tyrannical and unjust. Even Homer does much the same thing in the Iliad. At one point he has Thersites, a common soldier, lashing Agamemnon himself with the tongue of truth, while at another we see him crying like a child beneath the blows of Odysseus' gilded sceptre. These apparent contradictions must be accepted at face value, for it must not be forgotten that while sceptred monarchs had the right to command, the story-teller's lyre was in the hands of the common people, and clashes were inevitable. It is significant that while rulers are depicted as being the equals of Ares in power and daring, the singer-poets did not create a single myth in which the god of war emerges victorious, but many in which he suffers defeat and humiliation.

As for the illustrations, we believe that a picture should speak for itself. Nevertheless, we should like to say a few words about them.

We had to choose between two schools of thought. According to the one —and this is a line taken by many illustrators— we would have been obliged to remain faithful to the classical originals, chiefly vase-paintings, working in two dimensions, without perspective and with sparing use of colour. The other approach dictated that we use a modern style, and this we have preferred — but with one important prerequisite: that the picture, like the text, must itself be mythology. Thus, while keeping to the classical line, we have added a few elements of perspective where this seemed absolutely necessary. In one respect, however, we felt that we must have absolute freedom, and that was in the colouring. In our opinion, it was precisely the bright colours we have used which would give our work the fairytale air which the myths have to the modern reader's eye. For the ancients, in contrast, mythology was religion. For them the gods were real and not mythical beings. To us mythology is something else — a collection of wise and charming stories which shine like a bright fabric of the imagination from out of the depths of the centuries. It is for this reason that we have tried to illustrate this series with colour alone, or rather, by weaving harmonious contrasts of colour, but never forgetting that our theme is Greek mythology.